The Donkey of Gallipoli

A True Story of Courage in World War I

Mark Greenwood

illustrated by Frané Lessac

CANDLEWICK PRESS
CAMBRIDGE, MASSACHUSETTS

Jack and Billy grew up in the back alleys of South Shields, England, where a river carried great ships out to sea.

During summer vacation, they led donkeys along the beach for a penny a ride. From morning till twilight, they paced the seaside trail, whistling tunes for passengers balanced on the donkeys' backs.

In the winter, Jack delivered milk to support his family. With a ring of his bell, he worked the cobbled streets, taking payment with his frozen fingers. In the harbor, freighters and tugs sounded off with toots and whistles. Jack dreamed that one day he would sail away on a great adventure.

"There's no need to worry," he told Billy. "I won't forget you."

At seventeen, Jack signed up as a stoker on a ship bound for Australia.

He beat his way through the bush.

He cut cane and rode the boundary of a cattle station.

He labored in the coal mines, then joined the gold rush.

But Jack never dug a fortune from the ground.
Instead, he returned to the sea. Down in the
bowels of a steamship, Jack fed the furnace.

I wish I were home, he thought.
Every bird likes its own nest.

Jack was enjoying a spell ashore in Australia when he heard
the news that England and Germany were at war. He was quick
to enlist in the army. It offered a chance to do his duty for king
and country—plus a ticket home quicker than planned.

Jack trained as a stretcher bearer, but the troops sailed for Egypt, not England, as he'd hoped. In the shadow of the ancient pyramids, soldiers practiced for battle. Jack marched through the desert and treated mock-wounded at an aid station pitched among the palms.

When Turkey entered the war, British commanders drew up plans to launch an invasion on the Gallipoli Peninsula.

You'll find out where I am when the Australians make a start, Jack wrote to his mother.

On a moonless April morning, a fleet of destroyers steamed toward the Turkish coast. Steel hulls formed a line facing the landing point. Jack climbed down a rope ladder into a crowded rowboat.

Pale-faced soldiers prayed silently as the convoy approached the rugged, clay-faced cliffs. Enemy gunfire sparked from the scrub-covered ridges.

Jack's heart pounded. "I wish I were home in good old Shields," he whispered.

At dawn, the boats grounded on a pebbled seabed.

Turkish machine guns snickered, whipping up spouts of water.
Jack felt the zip of a bullet pass by his head. He tumbled into
the icy Aegean Sea and waded to shelter beneath an overhang.

Soldiers stormed the beach under orders to secure higher ground.
They fixed bayonets and charged up the razor-backed ridges.
Enemy artillery exploded overhead, showering the cove
with fiery shrapnel.

Exposed to bullets and bombs, Jack edged along narrow tracks
to evacuate a constant stream of wounded to lifeboats that
lined the shore.

The first-aid station at Hell Spit was unprepared for the mounting
casualties. Stretchers soon became a scarce commodity.

Jack was responding to a cry for help when he came upon a donkey cowering in a gully of pines. A shell burst high above, spitting out a hail of metal. Jack ignored the concussion of artillery and crawled across the shell-torn ground.

"Bless you, little fella," he whispered into a long fluffy ear, and he christened his frightened friend "Duffy."

Within reach of a dozen enemy rifles, a soldier raised his bloodied arm. Jack leaped over craters gouged into the battlefield, dodging shot and shell.

"It doesn't do to linger in nasty spots like this," he said. Jack gently lifted his patient onto the donkey's back.

He guided Duffy with a lead rope fashioned from field dressings and picked his way down the stony ravine.

That was the first of many brave rescues. In sunshine or drizzling rain, Jack Simpson marched up Shrapnel Valley with Duffy by his side. They made twelve to fifteen trips each day, carrying water to thirsty troops and returning with a soldier straddled over the donkey's back.

At night, Jack guided Duffy by lantern light down the zigzag track and camped with an Indian artillery unit. The Sikh gunners named him *Bahadur*—meaning "Bravest of the Brave."

Simpson and his donkey earned the admiration of all who watched them work. The colonel decorated Duffy's forehead with a Red Cross armband. "You're worth a hundred men to me," he said.

On the morning of May 19th, Turkish forces launched a fierce assault. It seemed a miracle that anyone could survive when the air was hazy with lead.

"Snipers are busy in the gully ahead," warned a soldier. "It's hot as blazes up there."

"I'll be all right," said Jack with a wave. "Have breakfast ready when I get back."

With the rising sun behind him, a Turkish soldier took aim
and slowly squeezed the trigger. His target was leading a
donkey up a steep incline at the junction of Dead Man's Ridge.

The bullet struck Jack in the back and passed through his heart.
Fellow soldiers dragged their friend to the side of the track,
and word passed down the line.

Battle-weary men were misty-eyed when Duffy trudged down the valley alone. Indian gunners risked their lives to gather a wreath of poppies to decorate a wooden cross. A hush descended over the battlefield. In the maze of terraced dugouts, candles flickered like evening stars on the night Jack Simpson was buried at Hell Spit.

Jack rescued more than three hundred men during twenty-four days. Among them was an English soldier who grew up in the back alleys of South Shields.

"There's no need to worry," Jack had called out over the stutter of gunfire. "I won't forget you."

Jack supported the wounded man to prevent him from slipping off the donkey. With Duffy trotting by his side, Jack smiled, whistled a tune, and led Billy through the valley of death.

Lest we forget . . .

JOHN SIMPSON KIRKPATRICK
a.k.a. Jack Simpson

NICKNAMES:		
Jacky, Simmo, Murphy, Scotty, Simmie		
DATE AND PLACE OF BIRTH:		
July 6, 1892, South Shields, County Durham, England		
MILITARY UNIT:		
3rd Field Ambulance, Australian Army Medical Corps		
NUMBER:	202	RANK:	Private
DATE AND PLACE OF DEATH:		
May 19, 1915, Shrapnel Valley, Gallipoli, Turkey		
CEMETERY:		
Gallipoli 30, Beach Cemetery, Anzac Cove		

Jack spoke with a Geordie accent, which identified him as someone born within sight of the river Tyne, in northeast England.

BILLY LOWES

Able seaman William (Billy) Lowes joined the Nelson Battalion, Royal Navy. His division, sent to reinforce the Anzacs (Australian and New Zealand Army Corps), landed on April 29th. Four days later, he was wounded.

Lapsing in and out of consciousness, he remembered being taken down to the beach aid station on a donkey.

"We used to play together as children, but I did not recognize Jack at the time," he said. "Shot and shell were flying all around when Jack struck across my path and brought me in on his donkey."

MASCOTS

The Australian soldiers believed that kangaroos and other animals would bring them good luck.

When they traveled abroad to fight in the war, they brought mascots from home to raise their spirits and help them feel less homesick.

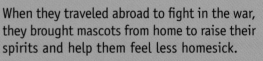

THE DONKEYS

Jack sometimes used other donkeys to give Duffy a rest. He gave them a variety of names, including Murphy, Abdul, and Queen Elizabeth. But Duffy was his favorite. At a ceremony at the Australian War Memorial on May 19, 1997, the Purple Cross was awarded posthumously to all the donkeys for exceptional work performed while under continual fire at Gallipoli.

THE TURKS

From April to December 1915, more than one million Allied and Turkish soldiers fought on the battlefields of Gallipoli. One in two was either wounded or killed. The people of Turkey know it as the Battle of Çanakkale.

The Turkish soldiers defended their homeland with much courage and honor, and the Australian and New Zealand soldiers regarded their opponents with great respect.

In some places the trenches were so close that the Anzacs could hear the Turks singing songs in the evening. Sometimes the soldiers exchanged food and gifts.

GENERAL MUSTAFA KEMAL ATATÜRK

The Battle of Çanakkale was where the great Turkish leader, General Mustafa Kemal Atatürk, led his troops to victory over the Allied forces. Atatürk expressed the bond between the soldiers from all nations with these famous words:

"Those heroes who shed their blood and lost their lives, you are now lying in the soil of a friendly country. Therefore rest in peace. There is no difference between the Johnnies and the Mehmets to us where they lie side by side in this country of ours. You, the mothers who sent their sons from faraway countries, wipe away your tears; your sons are now lying in our bosom and are in peace. After having lost their lives on this land, they have become our sons as well."

BABY 700

THE NEK

• QUINN'S POST

• STEELE'S POST

LONE PINE •

MONASH VALLEY

THE SPHINX •

PLUGGE'S PLATEAU

SHRAPNEL VALLEY

NORTH BEACH

HELL SPIT •

ANZAC COVE

AEGEAN SEA

N

ANZAC COVE, TURKEY, 1915

For the soldiers from all nations who fought and died at Gallipoli

Special thanks to Chris Goddard and the staff at the Australian War Memorial Museum; the staff at South Shields Public Library; the West Australian Army Museum; and Gary Hayes for expertise on military uniforms.

This project has been supported by ArtsWA in association with Lotterywest, and assisted by the Australian Government through the Australia Council, its arts funding and advisory body.

Australian Government

Australia Council for the Arts

First U.S. edition 2008

Library of Congress Cataloging-in-Publication Data

Greenwood, Mark, date.
The Donkey of Gallipoli : a true story of courage in World War I / Mark Greenwood ; illustrated by Frané Lessac. —1st U.S. ed.
p. cm.
ISBN 978-0-7636-3913-6
1. Kirkpatrick, John Simpson, 1892–1915. 2. World War, 1914–1918—Campaigns—Turkey—Gallipoli Peninsula.
3. World War, 1914–1918—Medical care—Australia. 4. Donkeys—War use. 5. Australia. Australian Army.
Royal Australian Army Medical Corps—Biography. 6. Gallipoli Peninsula (Turkey)—History, Military.
7. Soldiers—Australia—Biography. I. Lessac, Frané. II. Title.
D568.3.G74 2008
940.4'26—dc22   2007032525

10 9 8 7 6 5 4 3 2 1

Printed in China

This book was typeset in Cheltenham.
The illustrations were done in gouache.

Candlewick Press
2067 Massachusetts Avenue
Cambridge, Massachusetts 02140

visit us at www.candlewick.com

Sources:
Adam-Smith, Patsy. *The ANZACs: The Classic Account of the Men Who Gave Birth to the Legend.* Victoria, Australia: Penguin, 1991.
Bean, C. E. W. *Official History of Australia in the War of 1914–1918. Volume I: The Story of ANZAC.* Sydney, Australia: Angus and Robertson, 1921.
Benson, Irving C. *The Man with the Donkey: John Simpson Kirkpatrick, the Good Samaritan of Gallipoli.* London: Hodder and Stoughton, 1965.
Buley, E. C. *Glorious Deeds of Australasians in the Great War.* London: Andrew Melrose, 1915.
Cochrane, Peter. *Simpson and the Donkey: The Making of a Legend.* Victoria, Australia: Melbourne University Press, 1992.
Curran, Tom. *Across the Bar: The Story of Simpson, the Man with the Donkey.* Queensland, Australia: Ogmios Publications, 1994.
———. *Not Only a Hero: An Illustrated Life of Simpson, the Man with the Donkey.* Queensland, Australia: ANZAC Day Commemorative Committee, 1998.
Hamilton, John. *Goodbye Cobber, God Bless You.* Sydney, Australia: Pan Macmillan, 2004.
King, Jonathan. *Gallipoli Diaries: The ANZACs' Own Story Day by Day.* New South Wales, Australia: Kangaroo Press, 2003.
Moorehead, Alan. *Gallipoli.* South Melbourne, Australia: Macmillan, 1989.
Robertson, John. *ANZAC and Empire: The Tragedy and Glory of Gallipoli.* Victoria, Australia: Hamlyn, 1990.

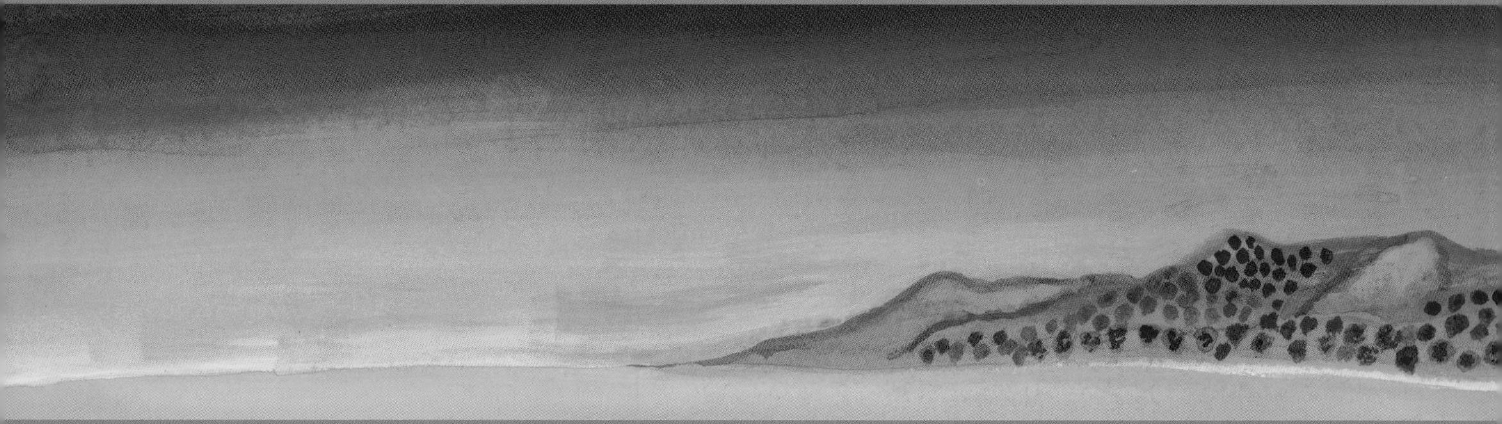